ANGELS AND SAINTS

ANGELS
&
SAINTS

George Otto Simms

FOUR COURTS PRESS

The typesetting for this book was
produced by Gilbert Gough Typesetting, Dublin for
Four Courts Press, Kill Lane, Blackrock, Co. Dublin.

BRITISH LIBRARY CATALOGUING IN PUBLICATION DATA

Simms, George, 1910-
Angels and saints.
1. Christian doctrine. Angels
I. Title
235'.3

ISBN 1-85182-042-6

ACKNOWLEDGMENT
The author wishes to thank the
Editor of the *Irish Times* for
permission to publish these articles
in a modified form.

Printed by
The Guernsey Press Co. Ltd.,
Guernsey, Channel Islands

Contents

All Angels

ngels have always seemed more distant than saints. They are less personal and names are found for only a few of them — Michael, Raphael and Gabriel. In our imagination we picture an anonymous multitude of angelic hosts, arrayed rank upon rank. The saints come readily down to earth; homely saints and even national saints, we dare to call groups of them. Angels, however, are too inapprehensible for the clutching. Their appeal is but spasmodic. Children and heroes claim their guardian angels and find in them protection against the power of evil and darkness. We blame the artists of a certain period for giving us an indelible picture of angels in the lump, sub-human rather than supernatural, with their weak and wan faces.

Yet angels people the world of spirit. They are invisible, intangible. For heaven is not a dull state of life, a mere condition of existence, but a scene of activity, varied and harmonious, to quote Walter Hilton, 'a favourable fellowship of blessed angels.' Their wings symbolise activity and speed, their ranks order, their number majesty and ready service, their hosts bring protection and raise to the heights the humblest act of virtue and obedience.

'The angels keep their ancient places
Turn but a stone and start a wing'.

They keep us in our place, too. For they serve to remind

us of the futility of meeting God on our own terms, of protecting our selfish wishes and passing them off as the will of God. Yet the very angels which bid us keep our distance radiate the power and love of God through every obscure corner of life. The *Gloria in excelsis* sung by angels at the birth of Christ tells us of the chief end of man.

They are messengers. Their higher service assures us who are on earth that heavenly life is not intermittently monotonous. They admit us to a view of the world invisible and bid us understand that the struggle with sin and the problem of suffering are not confined to this world, nor is their solution to be found at our level. The angels widen our horizons and bring us face to face with the wonder, majesty and holiness of God. Cherubim and seraphim join with apostles, prophets, martyrs and the holy church through all the world in a 'Te Deum' of continuous praise and adoration. Heaven and earth are linked; service continues in heaven, adoration must have its place upon earth.

Angels, ascending and descending on the ladder of Jacob, told of the way of exchange, of earth crammed into heaven, of the two worlds to which the mature must own that they belong. A place for this heavenly company is gratefully found by those who link all life with God and join the service they give on earth with his service on high.

Chariots of fire and heavenly ladders indicated the bridging of the heavenly will with the very earthy problems of wars, oppression and poverty which all are called upon to face with a message of hope and judgment. Angels, thousands of them, are messengers; thus the message is personal, lively, with an incalculable authority accompanying it.

Yet by their very number and order they have power to

reflect the many-splendoured creation of the holy and un-divided Lord of heaven and earth. Ranged in a hierarchy of thrones, dominions and powers, they emphasise the movement and harmony of those who render God service in the heavens. Angelic behaviour, so far from suggesting folded hands and lowered eyes, is concerned with burn-ing and cutting, firing and fighting. The war in heaven is spiritual combat between good and evil; ministering angels purge and cleanse as they respond to God's ordering and declare his glory.

That practical statesman, the prophet Isaiah, had a vision of angels and his own shortcomings were forcibly brought to mind when the feelings of his country weighed heavily on him. The sound of a voice from the heights, the whirring of winged seraphim, the misty cloud and a sense of holiness filled the picture forcing him to relate his life, both private and political, to God's way and wisdom, and to go out into the world of problems and possibilities which he had been sent to serve with quite an 'other' vision of its meaning.

The problem of communicating is a pressing one for every age. The theologian and the physical scientist alike have difficulty in making themselves understood. Every device is used to convey something of the meaning of a new invention or an indescribable experience. Sounds, imagery, illustration, comparisons, symbols are all brought into action. Yet still there is the sense of in-adequacy about the description. The words which relate a spiritual experience may easily be picked to pieces and caricatured by any sceptic who will not see. Consequently, angels also are often dismissed by the unthinking as nothing more than pretty material for a nursery frieze or the conventional *sine qua non* in a stained glass window.

The angels which find mention in the Bible are not such impossibly incredible creatures as the incredulous might suppose. They are seldom pictured as winged and wispy. They do, however, appear to accompany a spiritual event of moment and significance. At the birth of Christ there is a proclamation from the heavenlies of that unique occurrence. In our Lord's lonely ministry, angels attend him; their presence brings protection and divine assurance. At the empty tomb, the angelic presence turns an apparent absence into an abiding companionship, and banishes dismay from fearful hearts.

At these crucial moments in Christ's life, the writer of the Gospel, and the reader, too, became aware that their world had been invaded by powers which were spiritual and supernatural.

Angelic talk helps us to appreciate the power of God and the love of God; the guardian angel speaks of a power that strengthens; Christ in the loneliness of Gethsemane and in the earlier throes of temptation was still in touch with God's protection and the spiritual resources that appeared to be challenged. The conflict suggested by the figure of Michael the archangel overcoming the evil opposition is a message for our day.

The awareness of God's presence at worship in the company of angels and archangels helps us to receive the message and find the meaning. There is a message also in the struggle and the wrestling here below. Christians in their creeds are not called upon to formulate any definite belief about angels. But throughout the Bible angels are frequently mentioned; they provide atmosphere for events which are no ordinary happenings. Scholars have theologised about the nature and function of angelic beings; but beliefs about their way of life are not of first importance. Their existence and their operations, however, help us to appreciate the Creator's world, to understand its harmony and design.

Angels are remembered together with Michael the arch-angel. These beings are the message. The content of their mission is our primary concern. We do not count heads in the heavenly host but the cumulative effect of this com-munication of spiritual life and activity to us here on earth overwhelms us. We are right to worship and adore the Lord of heaven and all creation on Michaelmas day.

The message is personal. Answers to prayers are not written; they are heard in reason's ear, perhaps, or in the deep heart's core. Angels emphasise this personal an-nouncement of the message. Voices often describe the prayers we hear, the messages that are sent, the inter-pretation of what is essentially cryptic at times and always mysterious. The angels' message is alive and compelling when it comes from God. It is not surprising that we think of it in moving, lively terms. We speak of winged words when we sense that they get through to us with a flight that is sure and true.

The message is delivered at a place of meeting. There is receiving and responding in the life of spiritual com-munication. The giving of the message and the delivery of it are personal. Angels are encountered. On a journey, in a dream, with a vision, angelic ministrations look for receptiveness and co-operation from those for whom they are intended. Places have atmosphere. Danger and peace-

11

fulness: both can provide the setting for a spiritual direction.

Service lies at the heart of the ancient commemoration of the archangel Michael and the myriad messengers clustered round his personality. It is true that the picture before our minds is out of this world, and therefore baffling, mysterious, and all too easily dismissed as impossible. Yet, this heavenly scene is of considerable earthly use. The full meaning of service emerges from this vast, incomprehensible setting; the timelessness of the smallest act of generosity and self-sacrifice is perceived when the perspective is as wide as the heavens.

Small pieces of practical service, which sound cheap enough, such as the cup of cold water and the small coins of the widow, become permanently, and indeed eternally significant when understood, not merely as first aid, or as a conventional response to an appeal, but as loving and caring service.

There is grandeur in the word. The Michaelmas message clothes service with a rich dignity. There are no menial overtones when the serving is prompted by the spirit shown when Christ washed his disciples' feet. No touch of slavery entered that kind of ministry; the humility and the devotion came spontaneously from the will that graced the deed.

The disciples slowly grasped the message; the washing of their feet by their Lord and master illustrated what no words could adequately express, that work was not drudgery, labour was not degrading; a chore could cease to be a tedious task and become transformed into dedicated service.

Michaelmas seeks to express, not in words only but in powerful imagery, the meaning of service, given to God and creation. The season marks the beginning, for us, of winter programmes, the opening of term for schools and colleges; the law-court sittings bear the name of Michaelmas; a spirit of service is in the air. The prophets of biblical times, receiving their message for delivery to the people for whom they had a special concern, had a vision of God's nearness; they heard a call to service; they described the experience pictorially, artistically, as they saw the task assigned to them and discovered their vocation. Wings and voices indicated spiritual activity of a high order.

If we drain the language of prayer and worship, depriving it of colour, warmth and wonder, we find our words run dry and our imagination grows dull. The poets can phrase what we could never express; we welcome their help in communicating through language what at certain moments we feel, but cannot speak. Artistic buildings also, when entered, can provide us with a setting of awe and majesty. In such ways we struggle against the temptation to make God in our own image. We need on countless occasions to be cut down to size.

The modern art of Coventry's cathedral retains the ancient symbolism of God's activity in its dedication to the archangel. The bright transparency of glass, engraved with shadowy, flying figures, proclaims a dynamic faith. The graceful movements suggest the harmonies of faithful living, the rhythm of God's mighty operation, and the descent of the Spirit upon the world to transform and to purify.

Even the revised and modernised liturgies have not banished the mention of angels. Reference to them has survived into the age of space-travel for more than purely cosmetic reasons; there is still the urgent need to retain the sense of wonder, shock, amazement and astonishment in our earthy attempts to respond to God's goodness and power.

Words of reasoning and argument are too feeble to express much spiritual experience. Poetry, music, paintings and architecture can help to convey the mysterious, yet lively, meaning of our world's 'otherness'. If angels are apart and remote, they have a message, a ministry, and an influence which invade our life and raise our sights as we seek to view these invisible enrichments of our humdrum, prosaic conditions of existence.

In these days angels appear to many to be childish or archaic. Perhaps the influence of art and imagery has left us unenthusiastic about these weird creatures and we feel that we would prefer to leave them in 'their ancient places'. Yet absence of interest in this order of created things may indicate a lack of spiritual sensitivity. A fallen angel is said to have whispered the lie that the others did not exist and that the world could continue happily under its own controls.

Michael and his angels symbolise the two-way service constantly available. 'Ever fit us by service on earth,' we sing, 'for Thy service on high'. The scriptures, also, tell the complex story of love and suffering, providence and trial. Apocalypse and history are intermingled with moral counselling and parable, within the Bible's covers. Michaelmas reminds us of a dimension in devotion and doctrine that we can ill afford to neglect. We see things more clearly when we are shown the mysteries. As Origen wrote of old: 'All scripture has a spiritual meaning, not all has a literal meaning.'

The Fore-runner

In a little village of vines and olives, John the Baptist was wonderfully born. So runs the tradition that tells of the birth to Elizabeth and Zacharias, the High Priest, when both were old. The salutation of Mary, the Mother of Jesus, to Elizabeth, while they looked forward to the birth of their children, took place in the hill country, north-east of Bethlehem, at Ain Karem, much visited by pilgrims today. June 24th is the birthday remembered; the Church of the Visitation, cared for by Franciscans, dedicated to Elizabeth, stands in the village.

There is a story about the date. Not only does it fall six months before Christmas since John was half a year older than his Master. It also suggests the longest day, and the days which follow begin to diminish in length, however imperceptibly. Saint Augustine sermonised upon this: 'John was born today', he wrote of June 24th, 'and from today the days decrease: Christ was born on the eighth of the kalends of January, and from that day the days increase.' Thus the very date which we are approaching was seen to symbolise the forerunner's words about Jesus himself: 'He must increase and I must decrease'.

John was more than a prophet. He prophesied in words like others of the line, but he himself was prophecy, while yet unborn and in the womb. Small wonder that his date has enjoyed continued prominence. Both his birth and his death had special meaning. Samuel and John, the first and last of the Bible prophets, have particular mention made in the Scriptures of their births and deaths. For John, the beginning to the end of life denoted witness, a consistent and disturbing witness.

This witness prepared the ground for the Christian Gospel. He proclaimed good news, he communicated home truths, he comforted the have-nots, he protested at every level of society against injustices and failures in duty. Some called him an Elijah, as Christ was later to be called Elijah, for there was a spirit of reform and renewal in his life and work. John had the leathered loin of the man of God whom he resembled in his calls to repentance and his uncovering of the sins of society: 'He opened drains and pointed at smells'.

This prophet used the usual conventional language about cutting away the dead wood of rules and obsolete administration. He attacked the privileged position of those who relied on the family prestige of 'the children of Abraham' and seemed unwilling to make their own contribution in their own time. His illustrations, when he preached, were like Isaiah's; he called his listeners names — vipers' offspring, burning chaff, barren trees; we are back in the dusty, rocky hill country that needs irrigation schemes and afforestation, and clamours for a new spirit of vocation and industry among the people. There is film material in the fiery personality of this 'lion roaring in the desert' on whose account the symbol of St Mark's Gospel in the illuminated manuscripts is the king of the animal creation.

The voice of the Baptist was a cry in the wilderness. Yet it was not as forlorn as the phrase might suggest. This lone voice sounded not entirely on deaf, unwilling ears but penetrated with power and precision to every part of society in this prophet's day.

Minority opinions are not to be despised. John's voice claimed respect among his listeners who, like those of other days, are too often swayed by weight of numbers, giving little heed to the quality of speech and the meaning of the message. This last prophet spoke with courage and thrust, knowing full well that in the new era his work would be replaced.

Yet in all he attempted he showed the humility of his personality. The message, not the man, dominated as he faced people in many walks of life and showed them what they needed and where they failed.

The strength of humility often goes unperceived. John's selflessness, together with his capacity for sacrifice, is displayed as he 'boldly rebukes vice, constantly speaks the truth, and patiently suffers for the truth's sake.' Humility is no synonym for feebleness or hypocrisy. The transparent sincerity provided its own argument and furnished consistent proofs of authenticity.

However trying some of the saints in the calendar may appear to have been, their names, coupled with their deeds and characters, remind us of the individual's influence upon public opinion and massive movements.

The biography of the Baptist is necessarily scanty. Sufficient, however, is known of him to impress upon us the need for preparation before any great endeavour is launched. The analysis of human need which he provided for religious leader, uniformed soldier, or ordinary citizen caught the conscience and introduced a healthy note of realism in the world of his day.

He worked for the root; it was not to be his lot to enjoy the fruit of his labour. The beheading of John the Baptist appeared to increase the confusion in the situation and to deepen the despondency of those who had hoped for better things.

Yet the way through the spiritual bewilderment was found in terms of suffering and practice. These losses created fresh gains that could never be defeated. John had a share in the work of peace and reconciliation, achieved without the laurels of conventional victory.

In his name, on his day, many dedicated people serve the community in the everyday hazards of life with a willingness to meet human needs with skill and voluntary aid. The eight-pointed cross of the Order of Saint John of Jerusalem has sustained over the years a spirit of selflessness and concern that was wonderfully born long ago in the Holy Land.

These eight points classify an ordered life of service in an organisation which finds fulfilment in practical, highly-skilled deeds of neighbourliness.

Triumphant qualities are symbolised at every point which encompasses the familiar shape of this cross. Long-term victories quietly and modestly won are the fruit of such ordered living. We may think of them in pairs: Humility, Compassion; Courtesy, Devotion; Mercy, Purity; Peace and Endurance.

On St John's Eve we reflect for a moment upon the selflessness and unobtrusiveness which lend distinction to the service of those who tomorrow will dedicate themselves afresh to their labours. Such voluntary work, with a noble tradition behind it, gives wide scope to all sorts of conditions in our community.

There is something attractively constructive and pleasantly workable about the voluntary services which they offer so readily to the community.

This solidarity in responsible living is marked by the affliction of the Cross and the eight points of self-giving. Those who find their inspiration in the black and white symbol become alive to the needs of others, spending and being spent in the service of God and man.

In *humility* they serve, without distinction, the by-standers in the crowd; with *compassion* they bring the spontaneous help that springs from discipline and human understanding to the weak and infirm. With *courtesy*, they restore confidence to the panic-stricken. In *devotion* to duty, their vigilance precedes activity and anticipates disaster. The *mercy* of the good Samaritan models their neighbourliness; the *purity* of dedication scorns any reward save that of knowing that they do God's will. The *peace* of control and inner discipline combined with the *endurance* of those who continue a good work until it be thoroughly finished can only be satisfactorily interpreted in terms of a cross.

The Christ born of Mary

I n the Book of Kells, a full-page illustration of the birth of Christ makes an impressive picture. Admittedly, there is an air of solemnity in this Nativity scene. The message from the vellum's page speaks to us not so much of a happy Christmas as of a momentous incident in the history of the world.

Mary, the mother of the Christ-child, holds the baby in her lap. There is an other-worldly atmosphere surrounding these two central figures. The beauty lies in the dignity of the event and rather less in its homeliness.

This interpretation of Christmas reveals, by contrast with later portrayals of the Virgin and Child, something distinctively Celtic in the spirituality of the period.

The mother's figure is majestic, haloed, and strongly protective. Seated on a throne, studded with jewels, she dominates her surroundings. There is a feeling of destiny, power and mystery in her achievement, presented in the purples and emerald-greens, colours which, although subdued, bring a touch of royalty and richness to the scene. The features of the mother, outlined in an icon-like style, bring to the Irish gospel manuscript that familiar strand of Eastern art which blends happily with Celtic styles of ornament in the West.

If Mary as mother is outstanding for her strength and caring concern, the babe, with one hand on her breast and another laid on her right wrist, is both dependent and yet, at the same time, strangely mature. The babe has no halo; beneath the long robe which covers his body, what appear to be two left feet emerge! An added mystery, not un-paralleled, I understand, in sacred art.

Angels surround the mother and child; their matching mauves and purples seem to summon us to a hushed silence. Christmas is a holy festival, but a happy time also; yet the mood of adoration triumphs over the occasional signs of joy and hilarity in the picture.

In the right-hand lower corner of the page, six human heads can be seen, with heads turned away and their gaze averted. The mighty impact of this wonderful birth has apparently overwhelmed them.

Liveliness and keen curiosity, on the other hand, can be seen in the twists and turns of the two angels in the lower part of the page. They peep from behind the mother's throne in their eagerness to see this thing that has come to pass. Within the elaborately decorated frame-work of the whole page, pairs of quaintly tumbling little men, ener-getic and gymnastic, express their joy through the solemn majesty of 'the word made flesh'.

Matthew

St Matthew's Day reminds us of a book and a man. The book stands first in the New Testament's collection of twenty-seven writings. Its opening words, 'The book of the generation of Jesus Christ', introduce the longest and the most elaborate of the Gospel narratives. Throughout Christendom the Gospel according to St Matthew holds a foremost place in the affections of believers and inquirers. It contains good news for the passer-by in the street. Some say that its plan is over-formal and its symmetry artificial. Perhaps, indeed, the sections were numbered and arranged to suit the ear as much as the eye, to aid the memory of the unlettered, to stimulate and edify worshippers when passages were read at public services. At any rate, the groups of blessings and woes, the arrangements of questions and answers, the imposing array of parables and discourses bring the truths of the Kingdom of Heaven to the reader's mind with a compelling vividness.

It appears that this account of man's salvation through Christ was phrased in Jewish terms for Palestinians; St Luke wrote more generally for Gentiles and the wider world. In the first Gospel the controversy rages on a narrower field as the old dispensation yields before the new. Out of the midst of argument, much of what is outworn and outmoded is set aside, whereas the best of the traditional and established ways of ethical and

22

religious custom is transformed, presented in a new way with an added and original force. E. V. Rieu, introducing his version of the Gospels, refers to the special impression which the handling of the prophecies in the first Gospel made upon his mind: 'An event B does not occur and so fulfil a prophecy A; it occurs *in order that* A may be fulfilled. And the prophecies are not uttered *by* but *through* the prophets. This is a stupendous perception. God makes a plan, which Jesus volunteers to carry out'.

This note of fulfilment rings through the entire Gospel. There is a smoothness combined with a maturity in the narrative which tells us little of the author, but rather serves to emphasise the completeness and perfection of the 'Kingdom of Heaven'.

What of the man whose name has been linked down the centuries with this Gospel? His anonymity is designedly preserved; his personality remains veiled. The message of the book is greater than its compiler. For long the authorship has been attributed to the mature and experienced middle-man who collected tax by the Galilean lake. There are no traces of the eye-witness in the written word. But the publican who turned disciple forsook all covetous desires in search of righteousness and his new Master's Kingdom. His obedience to a call may have inspired the wisdom of a later saying: 'The person who wants to be just must always put himself in the place of a buyer when selling, and a seller when buying. No injustice is more widely spread in our world than that which tries to get the most for what it gives and to give the least for all it gets.' With similar insight the first evangelist abandoned the realm of commerce for the Kingdom of God.

Nothing in detail is told in the scriptures about Matthew's approach to his new responsibilities, after he had been called. We do know, however, that he was a tax official in the imperial administration and that he walked out from his job one day, apparently without hesitation. His name figures in the Gospels and Acts some half-dozen times in all; his presence on the team of the disciples is clearly important: 'who he was' may have been more significant than 'what he did'! Matthew is one of the few among the Twelve who are labelled. Mention is made in the official list of the disciples of his former occupation, which for all we know may have been for him a genuine calling. Simon 'the zealot' was also labelled, as a politician, a partyman. Without a doubt, the Twelve consisted of a diversified fellowship, far from monochrome.

The names of the Twelve were often repeated in the early days, while the faith spread. Each person had a name which carried a particular responsibility and authority of commitment, obedience, and self-sacrifice. The great exception was Judas, whose place was officially taken by another.

If Matthew's dossier was meagre, his witness carried a weight and importance worth recalling every year. We think of 'who he was', in the employ of a feared and foreign authority; we are reminded of whom he worked with, as part of an oppressive system, with many opportunities for private profiteering and devious accountancy.

Then, we consider the step he took, without turning back, and we guess how much he gave up in terms of cash and personal power. If we admire his prompt response to the call, we wonder still more at the influence of Jesus who invited Matthew to use his experience of the world and its way in quite a different direction.

The Gospel narrative which bears Matthew's name contains a wealth of teaching about money, its use and abuse.

With a taxman on the team of the Twelve, Christian discipleship dealt realistically with the stewardship of income, the importance of being loving and giving rather than merely existing in misery and miserliness; the urgency of meeting human need and abandoning greed; the place of honesty in the buying and selling of life's commerce. Matthew is said to have collected the 'sayings' of Jesus on these money matters; with a new vision of generosity he carried abroad (perhaps to Ethiopia) his new policies. His name signified 'a gift' (Bede called him Donatus). He died a martyr's death.

Mark

St Mark's Gospel may be the shortest of the four, but increasingly the biblical scholars have rated its importance high. Through Mark we have not only an early source which supplies hard evidence of what comprised the life and work of Jesus. We are also aware that this evangelist was in close touch with St Peter, the leading apostle.

It seems probable that Mark wrote down his Gospel in Rome, shortly after Peter's death by martyrdom. We may date his book in the late 60s of the first century. In the next century there is a written fragment by one Papias which throws interesting light on Mark's method and style. Papias describes Mark as the interpreter of Peter, and adds that he wrote down all that he remembered of the things said and done by the Lord. Admittedly, as a writer he was not experienced enough to set out his narrative in orderly fashion after the manner of a professional historian. Yet his directness and unvarnished style have the genuine ring of truth. Papias wrote further: 'Mark made no mistake in thus recording some things just as he remembered them, for he made it his one care to omit nothing that he had heard and to make no false statement about it'.

Mark helps us to understand what a gospel really is. We can sense the oral background behind the written words. The gospel was live news. Before the record was written down, it was passed on from 'mouth to mouth'; through conversation and even whispers and storytelling in the community. Mark is humble enough not to claim authorship of what he had received and was deeply concerned to pass on. We admire his anonymity.

He does not write about the birth and childhood of Jesus but he plunges his readers headlong into the gospel. 'The beginning of the Gospel of Jesus Christ': that opening sentence brings us immediately to the good news.

He wrote in simple Greek; this was the 'common' language shared by many Mediterranean countries and Greek was widely spoken in Rome at the time. Mark's thinking, however, was coloured by oriental expressions and, now and again, words in Aramaic break through the Greek. Mark gives us the sense that he has captured the very sounds of the voice of Jesus, when he gives us original phrases that smack of the countryside of Palestine. The key-word 'Ephphatha' — 'Be opened' — sounds authentic and has added power, when Jesus cures the deaf. The gentle phrases 'Get up, little girl' — talitha cumi — have been treasured by many translators of St Mark's Gospel. The cry of desolation uttered by our Lord from the Cross is not easily forgotten: the anguish of the Aramaic version of the psalm has for long been a Good Friday memory: 'Eloi, eloi, lama sabachthani', 'My God, my God, why hast thou abandoned me?'

The Gospel that bears Mark's name falls into two parts: first, the events reported in quick succession: healings, miracles, parables, new light on the Kingdom. Before he opens the second half, the crucial question and answer involving Jesus and Peter mark a turning point in the story. Jesus says to Peter 'Who do people say that I, the son of man, am?' And the mighty answer, with which Peter commits himself to his master, proves to be a turning point in his life: 'Thou art the Christ, the son of the living God'.

The way is open for the concluding portion of the Gospel. It concerns the person of Jesus, who he is and the reason for which he has been sent into the world. Mark's passion narrative is realistic; his description of dark days and grim suffering is plainly told, with little embroidery. So too his language, written in apocalyptic style, about the coming doom that will befall Jerusalem, that famous spiritual centre, and the accompanying prophecy about the future.

Mark had the essentials of the gospel clearly pictured in his mind. More than ninety per cent of his written material was embedded in St Matthew's Gospel. Mark's urgency and succinctness may have pointed to his priority among the evangelists. He ends abruptly. There is both credibility and yet mystery in the manner in which he breaks off the account of Jesus's resurrection. 'They were afraid', he wrote, and left his readers in suspense. The future, it seemed, he gave over to them.

Luke

St Luke's name is still held in honour by the physicians. His festival in mid-October is celebrated in medical circles. Hospitals have been dedicated to him; the inspiration of his writings and his manner of interpreting the good news of Christianity continue to inspire not only the medical profession but all who are concerned for people's welfare and health.

This particular evangelist puts people first, as he writes in a style both sympathetic and compassionate. Dante called Luke 'the scribe of Christ's gentleness'. It is noticeable that he selects the parables of Jesus which concern the characters and personalities of individuals with a special emphasis. Less space is given to the parables which illustrate the growth of nature and the order of creation. Luke, with the skill of the artist and the literary writer, paints in memorable phrases scenes from human life. Many are pen-portraits; the good Samaritan, the unjust steward, the prodigal son, the Pharisee and the publican fill the gallery.

With economy of words and with a deep understanding of human reactions, Luke records the incomparable teaching of the Master. By tradition, this evangelist has been called 'the beloved physician'. Nothing conclusive can be drawn from his manner of describing sickness and disease, although he uses medical language with remarkable competence.

The emphasis he lays upon the healing gifts of Jesus, however, is certainly striking. The Gospel according to St Luke unfolds much for us about the meaning of suffering and the liberation which forgiveness brings to a life tied and bound by anxieties and feelings of guilt.

St Luke, a second generation Christian, uses language which already was becoming current in the early creeds of the Christian church. His ability to summarise not only the incidents in Christ's life, but the meaning of those incidents, lends a special maturity to his warm-hearted record of the gospel of love and justice. Luke was, they say, from Antioch in Syria, outside the borders of Israel. He wrote for a wide audience about a world religion. His language is sometimes formal, written in the style of an historian of those days; at other times, he uses every-day conversational phrases; always he aims at translating the Hebrew background of faith, culture, prophecy and tradition into terms that can be appreciated by the outsider.

The translators of St Luke's Gospel have often expressed their admiration for his literary skill. The account of the walk to Emmaus after the Resurrection has been called a model short story, in its structure and its climax. We are not surprised that the man, Luke, should be honoured as well. His version of the Gospel was chosen for combined study and shared reading among all the Christian traditions in Ireland in a recent year when the healing of sores and the longing for peace and mutual understanding were urgently pressing. His words and interpretations are still needed today.

Artist indeed is this Gospel-writer who also is the author of the Acts of the Apostles There is a unity and plan about the two-volume work associated with the name of the physician and evangelist who travelled as a missionary through the Mediterranean countries as the companion of St Paul. It has been said that the reader would understand St Luke's Gospel better, if he studied it in close connection with the Acts and separated it from the other three Gospels. For what the evangelist writes in his first volume is developed and brought to fulfilment in the second. The clue to the preaching of the Gospel is discovered in the life of the early church, not only in Jerusalem, but also in Samaria and in many other countries further afield.

Luke wrote for the wide world. He begins his Gospel with a scene in the temple, and in the temple he leaves the disciples, at the end of the great account of the mighty acts of God performed in the life of Christ. In his second volume, however, he takes those mighty acts from the temple at Jerusalem through the nations to the secular capital of the world and demonstrates that the power of the Spirit, which worked through Christ in Palestine, continued in the Christian community which was the Church universal.

This writer is thus an ecumenical figure. Writing for all the nations and not for one alone, he brings his Gospel to a climax with the triumphant Resurrection and Ascension, and makes this moment in the Christian story a link with all that is told in the pages of Church history. It is the story of a kingdom, without territory and without walls. It tells of triumph through and after suffering, of disaster followed by restoration. St Luke traces in his account of the birth, suffering, death and resurrection of the Lord of this Kingdom a path to glory. Outcasts find special mention as they are rescued. Strangers are received into the fellowship of the Kingdom after barriers are removed and prejudices overcome. The beloved physician sees in

31

the story of salvation which he edits a mighty work of healing and reconciliation. What was made plain in terms of the few in one country long ago has continued with power and purpose through human lives of every age. St Luke writes for us all; his words are balm for human sores.

He gives space, in his account of what Jesus began to do and to teach, to the considerable part played by women in the scenes depicted in his version of the Gospel. This does not mean that women find no mention elsewhere among the evangelists; Luke's emphasis, however, is both movingly realistic and markedly favourable when he includes in the drama the role of the women who were involved in what took place.

The portrait of the Mother of Jesus is painted with tenderness; when another mother calls her blessed, we discover new depths in the role of both Mary and Elizabeth in the Gospel's opening scenes.

The women in this third gospel of the New Testament display gifts of directness and intuition, often in the presence of less discerning male company, when Christ is among them. Initiatives that lead to practical action include the touching of a garment's hem, breaking a precious box of ointment, sweeping a room with a determination to find a lost coin, giving two mites for what they were worth, going early to the sepulchre, just in case. These instinctive responses and acts of faith left many male onlookers standing and give posterity examples of hope and obedience that will not easily be forgotten. Even if Luke records the often quoted warning 'Remember Lot's wife', even when he emphasises the fruitlessness of the women's weeping as Jesus journeys to crucifixion, the steadfast faith and patient readiness to respond form an important part of their ministry. The historian's style presents with the light and shade of the eyewitnesses' observations a gospel for all the people, for all time.

This evangelist seems to have specialised in the recording of those incidents in Jesus's life which had a homely human setting. No fewer than eighteen parables are found in his gospel narrative exclusively — they do not feature in the other three. As might be expected from the pen of him who was traditionally a physician, these parables are notably personal! Such studies in character as are found in the well-known good Samaritan, or the prodigal son, or the Pharisee and publican have a universal application. These short stories, packed with drama, speak to people, in every country and condition, of God's love, justice and mercy.

Many other distinctive events could be added to a Lucan anthology with samples of literary beauty and superb reporting. The language of medical therapy lends authenticity to the leprosy cases, professionally described; a concern for persons provides a wide selection of individual encounters with Christ the healer and comforter; Mary and Martha are both treated with understanding; strangers and Samaritans are seen to count. The passion and crucifixion of our Lord himself are presented in terms of a tragedy which proves creative, in a setting of ultimate triumph without any minimising of what had to be endured. The agony in Gethsemane has an artist as well as a historian to paint its meaning. Tolerance, patience and judgment are all included in this moving preface to the Cross.

The evangelist's version of the suffering, trial and crucifixion of his Master reveals the creative character of the tragic march of events which led to the Cross. Out of suffering came forth a love tested by pain and thereby deepened. Out of the religious and political conflict came an unexpected revolution, more profound than any social or national crisis; the revolution of ideas and values brought healing to individuals and peoples. The wholeness of life emphasised with Lucan vocabulary and style has attracted the medical profession to this way of thinking and this manner of commending a gospel of redeeming love.

Malcolm Muggeridge's portrait of Mother Teresa of Calcutta provides an example of the power of Christian gentleness in the face of fierce conditions of famine and personal deprivation. A handful of devoted workers showing Christian compassion under an outstanding leader can scarcely supply the needs of thousands, who are suffering, homeless and outraged. Yet in the book, *Something beautiful for God*, the care and respect shown for persons by this pioneer of relief for the spirits and bodies of multitudes shine out effectively in a very dark scene. This Teresa, from Yugoslavia, trained for a while in Rathfarnham, Dublin, fulfils a vocation in the place to which the refugees have fled in panic. Much of her work lies with those whose physical strength is ebbing fast. One of her concerns is that the victims of disaster should at least 'die within sight of a loving face'.

'Without our suffering', she has written of herself and her co-workers, 'our work would just be social work, very good and helpful, but it would not be the work of Jesus Christ, not part of the redemption'. There is a Lucan ring in such a statement.

John

Two days after Christmas, John the Evangelist is commemorated. Traditionally his death was martyrdom. He is remembered chiefly for his life. Yet his day follows hard on the feast of Stephen, the first martyr, who, as the sermon in Eliot's *Murder in the Cathedral* reminds us, illustrates the note of tragedy which sounded through the Lord's life from the beginning. John emphasises in his own life, and, in the writings linked with his name, the abiding and victorious nature of the love which came down at Christmas. St Stephen's Day spelt triumphant suffering; St John's Day triumphant love; the day after, triumphant innocence.

John lived close to our Lord; he leant on his breast at the supper; he was one of the little company of three at the end as they stood apart from the rest of the disciples. The Gospel appointed on his day recalls the scene as Peter, John and their Lord converse. William Temple described them: 'The Lord of Love; the disciple in whom self would be offered; and the disciple in whom self would be forgotten.'

John, as an expounder of love, drew with the genius of an artist a portrait of his Master which may not give the details of a full biography, but does succeed in interpreting for readers and believers the person of the Lord and Saviour. This fourth gospel is increasingly the subject of serious study in our time, for it is seen to be in its orderliness and its coherence not merely a bare report of words spoken and events as they occurred, but a convincing picture of the heart and mind of the central figure who lived, acted and spoke, as never man did before or after.

John orders his narrative, not to press an argument, but to illustrate with a succession of illustrations the main proclamation which he presented at the beginning: 'The Word was made flesh.' He does not call his Master the Word in the chapters which follow the first. But the Johannine signs and symbols draw out the meaning of the first grand chapter, the famous Christmas Gospel. The miracles for John are no mere wonderworks; their point lies not in benefaction, but in glorification. A sick man may be given relief by the miraculous touch, but He who touched him is given the glory.

John's message consists of the Gospel story told by three other evangelists, but his presentation is distinctively intimate, personal, mystical. The other evangelists tell us what the Kingdom of God is like; John lays stress upon the Son of God. He it is who records the discourses which comfort and console; the great '*I ams*' of the fourth gospel provide inexhaustible material for thought and contemplation: '*I am* the vine, the Bread, the Light, the Way, the Truth, the Life.'

When this John, who writes reflectively, at a date later than the others, interprets the death and passion of the Lord he loved, he shows with confidence and never-failing hope that his Master is in control of each event, however tragic, in which He becomes involved. The writer sees victory lying beyond the defeat; he knew that love was stronger than death.

St John's Gospel was called 'spiritual' by an admirer of his thought and style, as early as the second century of the Christian era. Yet 'spiritual' was not used by Clement of Alexandria as a word to suggest anything remote or detached.

There was nothing 'up in the air' or 'out of this world' about the writer who described Christmas in crisp short-hand as 'the Word became Flesh'. Before that, this evangelist had written 'the Word was God'.

In the Christian calendar, one of the Christmas days is dedicated to St John, the beloved disciple. He saw the meaning of Christmas with a spiritual insight, gained by love and a sense of God's nearness. No inn, no shepherd, no wise men from the east, no Herod, no details of the Christ-child's birth have a place in the record of John. The event, the happening, opens up the meaning of it all.

If there is simplicity in the sound of the shortest possible words, used to identify the best of Christmas gifts, we must not be deceived by the ease with which light, life, love, grace, and truth trip off the tongue.

We soon discover the grandeur and the glory of them, shining through every chapter of the Gospel. The signs of the saving acts are presented in a wonderful order.

The writer, who lived close to our Lord, displays the authentic character of his account. History and arch-aeology, so the scholars have revealed, provide with re-markable accuracy the local scene in which eternal things are revealed. The pool of Bethesda's five porches has been excavated to show us the setting of a famous healing; the pavement of Gabbatha can be trodden over today to bring into the present the judgment of Pontius Pilate.

John emphasises the union of the divine and the human in the drama, as he writes. Light is contrasted with darkness; love overcomes evil in the world which Christ entered.

Three typical Johannine points make us joyful on his holy-day. First, the meaning of worship: it is spiritual, not locally tied; it continues; through it we learn to abide in love, and not break off. Jesus told the Samaritan woman that God was to be worshipped in spirit and truth. The well, beside which he spoke, is still there.

Again John provides a telling picture of work seen as service. No drudgery, nothing demeaning, no formal conventions mark the washing by Jesus of his pupils' feet. Humble work has a strength and a glory, despite the critics and the protests.

Lastly, John recognised that this powerful message of life and light could not be contained in any number of books that might be written. People, with all their human weaknesses and limitations, would continue to be the agents of the good news. The world was their readership.

The eagle has for long been the symbol of St John's Gospel; perhaps because, as has been said, the eagle alone of all living creatures can look straight into the sun and not be dazzled. So writes the well-known expounder of New Testament books, William Barclay.

He continues: 'John has the most penetrating gaze of all the New Testament writers into the eternal mysteries and the eternal truths and the very mind of God. Many people find themselves closer to God and to Jesus Christ in John than in any other book in the world'.

The essentials of faith are here expressed in very simple words. Yet when the writer discourses on light, life, and love, we find ourselves wrapped round by the mystery of these seeming simplicities. The author's purpose is summed up towards the end of his final chapter: 'so that you may believe that Jesus is the Christ, the Son of God, and that believing this you may have life through his name'.

James

The name of James is honoured as a saint and martyr, not alone in Spain, but throughout the Christian world. Far from local is the interest in this strong personality who was Christ's companion. His qualities of discipleship, obedience, unreserved courage and devoted loyalty are universally admired. The rough-hewn fisherman-son of Zebedee proved to be material for strong apostleship and tough sainthood.

In commemorating the saints, we find ourselves giving special thanks to God for the Spirit's working through a particular life in a certain place and age with all the limitations attached. The glimpses we have gained about the character and achievements of James the Great help us to have a more realistic, down-to-earth vision of the church's work and life. The church has produced martyrs, bold champions, heroes with a large capacity for suffering and hardship, such as James and many after him. In remembering this day and this name, we sense that we share a living brotherhood with many sons and daughters of God our Father; these have wrought great deeds and love in God's Kingdom and abide in him perpetually.

The outstanding quality of this James appeared to be his unquestioning obedience. This is recalled in the collect-prayer of his day. This 'leaving all and following' became a mark of true discipleship. The example of James and John, together with that of Peter and Andrew, was termed apostolic and evangelical. Their readiness to obey the call had an authentic ring about it; there was nothing fanciful and romantic here; instead, there was the surrender of an obvious livelihood and the abandoning of the security associated with home and parents, and a venturing forth into the uncertain, in response to an unmistakable and compelling invitation. Many a Christian has described the call to service in terms of the vivid lakeside-scene, where nets were being washed. Such has been the infectious quality of the group in which James was found.

James remained in the forefront of the followers of the Master. He was called, perhaps, not to be an outstanding leader or a remarkable individualist, but rather as a partner, a worker with others, one whose qualities needed supplementing or balancing in the business of proclaiming the good news of the freshly-found faith. He was there on the mount of Transfiguration; he was present, too, in the garden of the Agony; he and his partners were close to our Lord in the exalted moments no less than in the depths through which he had to pass. Only after such moving experiences could he give himself fully to the service that demanded suffering as well as obedience.

This son of thunder, with a holy fire in his belly, carried his boldness out into his apostleship in the world. We read of his death as an early martyr at the hands of King Herod Agrippa; James was slain, Peter was cast into prison. The mother of James had earlier sought a place for her son 'at the right hand' in God's presence in the life to come; she heard, in reply, something of the trial of suffering that comes before rewards.

This conversation, like so many ill-timed and unperceptive discussions, proved creative, since discipleship was seen more clearly to be service. The exercise of it included suffering. The right kind of ambition cared nothing for a place of distinction or an advancement in prestige. The spirit of calculation and the profit-motive did not interfere in this man's call. By the direct response of James the Apostle, God was glorified.

His thunderous words of bold faith and righteous indignation brought predicable suffering upon this uncompromising champion of the faith; is it too much to surmise that such types in the communion and fellowship about the throne of God are indeed in a position of significance 'at the right hand', the seat of praise and glory?

Thomas

He was not the usual kind of doubter. He was not of the sort which fumbles with ideas and toys with hesitations and hypotheses. He did not even enjoy his doubts. He was a literal-minded person, and perhaps somewhat gloomy, but his questions showed that he had difficulties; and his waverings were those of one who is well on the road of faith and is doing some hard thinking. Doubts, for such, have been neatly termed 'growing pains'.

Thomas gave his loyalty to his Lord at an early stage, and in the lists of the disciples he is numbered with the twelve. His pilgrimage stands out distinctively in the record of the disciples' doings, and we learn to admire him the more for the manner in which he faced up to his troubles. Growth in discipleship was for him painful and heart-searching. When he did express belief in the risen Lord, his whole-hearted exclamation 'My Lord and my God' outstripped any other profession of faith that had been made. The doubter not only found his faith, but shouted it out aloud in no uncertain terms. It is not surprising that an early tradition held that he was an effective and thrustful missionary who carried the message of the Resurrection eastwards to India.

Three incidents in St Thomas's life, as recorded in St John's Gospel, form an illuminating pattern of his spiritual experience. In each case we see the thinker tested.

When news is brought of the death of Lazarus, Thomas does not stay to question, nor yet does he consider the case ended. He is the one who volunteers to act and, speaking with an unconscious touch of prophecy, he makes history with a statement which shows that ready action stimulates faith, whereas wavering delay nourishes doubts. 'Let us go also,' he says, 'that we may die with him'. It was not a time for whys and wherefores.

A second incident shows us the doubter with his thoughts. He is present as our Lord discourses. 'Whither I go ye know the way,' the Master says, Thomas is not so sure. There is something logical in his reaction; how could he say that he knew the way if he did not know the goal to which it led? Those who are path-finders are exhorted to make certain that they know clearly their destination, tracing the route on the map, before they set out. In spiritual adventures, however, things are different. Faith persists when knowledge ends. The way in this case was the Master; the loyalty of trust and unquestioning devotion could be given to him who was 'the way' by those who were completely ignorant of the Master's destiny. Faith was, in short, a loyalty to a person rather than a carefully drafted set of beliefs.

The classical doubting scene after the Resurrection tests supremely the faith of Thomas. He was, like many others, looking for a sign, for tangible proofs. These were withheld. Then, after an agonizing interval, he joins his fellow-disciples, on the first day of the week, with the doors shut; he hears the familiar sound of the greetings of peace; he was shown the marks and could have touched the wounded hands and pierced side. He had no need now to touch; his faith had stood the test, his doubts were resolved; his arguments and questions were answered by himself in words of acclamation — 'My Lord and my God.' The doubting disciple thereafter gained fame as a missionary-minded apostle.

Philip and James

The first day of May in the Christian calendar is dedicated to two disciples of Jesus; Saint Philip and Saint James are paired off for commemoration. They have not the prominence enjoyed by some others of the twelve. Their readiness to follow, their loyalty, and their partnership of service are nevertheless worthy of remembrance. If May Day is more recently associated with work, the same day for the Christians has most practical overtones.

It is on this day that faith in Christ is spelt out in three words of one syllable — the Way, the Truth and the Life. The disciples in their questions drew out from their master's teaching the essentials of the faith they found and followed. They left their homes and work and went after the one who had called them; as they went and remained in his company, they became convinced of his authority and of the claims he made for himself and for them; this was their life, to be with him, and to be ready to die for him.

The *Way* was an early name for the faith which is most practical in its expression. It is a faith which is learned by believing and by acting on the belief. The disciples learned by walking with Jesus; the early Christians learned by moving out to meet people in neighbourliness. They saw faith as action and life as a journey. Their instruction was given as rules for a road. Their life was so far from being static and stagnant consisted in active pilgrimage and sojourning. The Christian is always *in via, en route*.

The *truth* seemed to be with the disciples as they kept in touch with their Master. Jesus was truth. Christianity is described, in short, as Christ, since he revealed the will and purpose of God. God was in Christ. Thus the truth was discovered by following, obeying, serving and loving. The truth was not written or expressed in words. It was grasped by knowing the truth, as a disciple knows a master, or a friend a friend. It was by doing the truth in love that the disciples became men with a message, apostles of truth.

The *life* was more than biological. There was a distinctive word for life which denoted more than breath and heart-beat. Christianity is of this world as the birth of Christ declared; it is a way and a truth for this world. In many ways, its interests are most material. On May Day, the Christians show their concern to bring abundant life into drab existence, to work for the material well-being of the homeless and the hungry. To live alongside the lonely and the despised is but one illustration of the meaning of the life of love which the Christians discovered, when they began to be disciples.

Bartholomew

The name of the saint was included in the famous list of twelve. His name is not forgotten; his personality, however, is veiled. We know little of what he did. We give thanks for what he was. A disciple, a martyr, a special selection for a mighty task, Bartholomew inspires us for the right reasons. He did not leave behind a biography; a gospel, which bore his name, did not qualify for inclusion among the books of the New Testament, but was declared apocryphal. Yet he is honoured as part of the great fellowship which spread the faith, north, south, east and west in dangerous, precarious days.

Bartholomew's name has a distinctive ring. There is music in its vowels. For a long time his was a frequent Christian name in Irish families; Bart and Parthalon recall this early apostle. Hospitals and churches drew inspiration from his compassion and faith. We know that he went out, one of a pair, to express through life and example the love for people which his Master incomparably showed. Two by two, these disciples discovered their ability to put flesh on the abstract qualities of unself- ishness and courage. Through their lives, in their deeds, and by their deaths, they preached the best kind of sermons. Bartholomew left us nothing in writing. He reminds us where true valour lies; his priorities were right; he was one of those who gave themselves that others might learn life's essential worth and value.

One French Christian of this century took that name Bartholomew and turned the associations of cruelty and shame which for centuries had darkened St Bartholomew's day into a venture of faith and repentance. The Abbé Paul Couturier, in his longing for unity, saw that a new effort to repair the damage done by Christians of all traditions through persecutions and bitter controversies could only be successful if hearts were changed and responsibility for past outrages were genuinely and mutually shared. St Bartholomew's eve for him, who knew his country's history well and understood the causes of some persisting religious bitterness, became nothing less than a springboard from which to make a new start in friendly and reconciling relationships among Christians deeply estranged. By himself sharing the blame and shouldering some of the responsibility for that historic tragedy on a night to remember, he encouraged others no longer to condemn the sins of opponents and outsiders but to repair the breaches and bridge the divisive gaps by admitting their own faults and sins of failure too often neglected, when eyes were averted, and minds did not want to know. The Abbé's prayer of sorrow and his request for forgiveness changed the whole tenor of honest intercession for unity. St Bartholomew's day became a starting point for a new approach.

Andrew

A practical saint is the first on the list. The Christian calendar begins with Andrew. A fisherman by tradition and occupation, he launched out not only from the lake that gave him his livelihood, but also from the country of his culture and inheritance. He was ever ready for a new start.

He is remembered as the disciple who pointed to the only source of supply he saw in the desert when the crowd on a famous occasion grew weak with hunger. The lad with the five loaves and two fish, at the prompting of Andrew, helped something small and rationed to become fantastically great. Such initiatives, however slight, mark in the disciple both faith and expectancy, the sequel of faith. Such a one is counted in Christian thinking as the prototype of the missionary. His activity and his practical commonsense combined with his obedience to a call and his keen sense of human fellowship have inspired Christians of every age. Like Andrew they travelled, they reached out, they found others and brought them to Christ. We know little of his life story, but the glimpses given in the Gospels are compelling and attractive. He was not ashamed to be himself, even if he is found more often with others than alone. He attempted what was within his reach and found a vocation in the pursuit of what he had been equipped to do.

Voluntary service overseas, warriors in the battle

against want and waste find inspiration in the practical discipleship of an Andrew. His faith, with words passing into deeds, commends itself to a world, weary of argument. The modern missionary may find himself, more often with a tractor than a tract, serving people to whom he feels committed through a shared humanity. With technical skill and a concern for the welfare of others, he finds his mission in bringing aid through trade in under-developed countries. This identification of the missionary with the people whom he serves, be he evangelist, agricultural specialist, teacher, medical or administrator, becomes in Christian terms, Andrew-like. He is there at moments of opportunity and decision. He gives the start to projects that increase and develop with faith and vision. Through him, God's work is done in people, beyond ordinary expectation, past human knowing. In such lives we see the meaning of grace to be the love of God in action.

On St Andrew's day honour is paid to the saint not only in Russia and Scotland, countries where his influence is intimately felt, but also throughout a worldwide Church which recognises the inspiration which the Galilaean fisherman gave to the great evangelising movement of passing the Word along the line to the mighty human race. He who said 'There is a lad where, which hath five barley loaves and two small fishes' had learned the secret of making a hopeful beginning with the resources available. He perceived the limitless possibilities possessed by the grace of God, once it begins to work upon nature. Andrew did not expect a sudden act of God to solve his problem; his offering of a little was made in trust and expectancy, and when God transformed the natural offering, there was a miraculous multiplying of the basic needs of life. Such wonderful expansion continued in a Church which

51

had its humble beginning amid a handful of unlettered disciples within the narrow confines of an upper room. Andrew with his well-known diagonal cross symbolises the costliness of making a new beginning in our life with Christ; he also reminds us of the worldwide extent of the spiritual Kingdom for which he fought with such practical resolve as a fisher of men.

Peter

On Saint Peter's day we remember a colourful character. Here is a personality which demands our attention; for he played a leading part in the formative years of the Christian church.

At first sight, he appears to be one of the surprising choices of Christ; it was by no means obvious that one of such a temperament would be able to carry through the work which was assigned to him. Our Lord's selection of men was not made after formal interview or examination; the choosing was much more personal. The personalities of his disciples deserve our constant study.

The sort who are called to continue work given to them to do must have their heart in that work. In devoting themselves to the cause, they need to do battle against self-interest and, furthermore, against misrepresentation. Unlike the successors and followers of emperors such as Alexander the Great and of the dictators of more recent times, the twelve found themselves appointed to tasks which have had results of lasting influence.

Their work has not died out. The twelve had their temptations and made human mistakes; but we have reason to believe that most of them grasped the point of their commissioning and ultimately were found faithful. The church they served was apostolic, built upon persons of varying talent and different texture.

Peter's weaknesses, as often happens in the history of leaders, received grim publicity. The traits in his character which suffered contempt were exposed and then treated; as a result, they were used for God's glory and not for man's shame. A bad temper, for example, can be redeemed and used for the passionate championing of a worthy cause; again, a blunder, committed early in life, may earn a sharp rebuke and help to lead a personality from self-conceit into a life of generous service. In some such way, Simon Peter's mistakes revealed the man to himself no less than to others. These falterings marked the prelude to a life of personal triumphs. He may not have had the academic gifts of a Paul nor the popular and ever attractive even-tempered patience and affection of a John, but with his rude speech and rough ways he was chosen for leadership and responsibility.

To his Master who gave him his vocation with the words 'Thou art Peter,' he had been given courage and confidence to say beforehand 'Thou art the Christ'. The glory of Peter's biography lies in his ability to break through the conventions of a dry-lipped morality and to give himself whole-heartedly to the new and wider business of fishing for men's souls. There was plenty of crude material for God's grace to work upon here. The finished portrait of one who was, it is said, willing to be crucified in his Lord's cause is a work of art which brings ever fresh inspiration to those who stand before it and ponder its features each anniversary day.

There was a time when Peter, with all his potential for leadership, was clearly short of faith; he found it hard to believe. At other times, his courage and sense of trust seemed to know no limits; he took risks and plunged into deep waters out of sheer devotion. Again, in spite of much questioning and challenging, he would supply the penetrating answer, scarcely aware of its source or meaning; he had the gift of reaching to the heart of the truths his Teacher constantly pressed home.

He listened carefully to the famous answer about forgiveness and the need to be continually forgiving, to the power of seventy times seven. The best lesson in this subject, however, was learned when the cock crew near an outer court, and the Lord turned and looked upon Peter. It was a hard lesson, never to be forgotten. John Donne helps us to remember it for our own needs: 'The eye of his Lord,' he wrote, 'lightened Peter's darkness'.

Donne elaborates: 'We hear of no blows, we hear of no chiding from Him towards Peter . . . the eye of the Lord lighted his darkness, the eye of the Lord lighted those three crusts of ice, which were grown over his heart in his three denials of His master.'

With hindsight, we perceive that this saint became dedicated, devoted and saintly by the hard and testing way of suffering, sinning and slipping. He had his mountain-top experience and found it good, although difficult to understand; doubts and perplexities also attacked him in dark moments. His Master warned him against saying 'never'; a warning for our times, no less.

Peter said 'never' at least three times; he declared that the killing of his Master and friend 'would never happen'; he protested at the thought of his Master doing him a service and showing him hospitality; Peter wanted to be the one to do the serving: 'You shall never wash my feet'. He had to learn to receive with a good grace. Over-confident, overflowing with zeal, he had cried, before the awful moment of denial, 'I will never fall away'. There is a lesson for us on the festival day of a saint who became what at one time seemed most improbable, a leader unshakeable in the faith, restored, renewed and rock-like. We should 'never' say never in these spiritual issues.

He was, as is recorded, on occasions, helplessly human. We warm to him on that account; experiences of our own, which we think are best forgotten, are strangely like his in those famous weaker moments, when he learned genuine discipleship.

We learn from him, who, in later days when the whole world seemed to be his responsibility, was sufficiently humble and realistic to declare, 'I am a man'. We learn about this great teacher when the arguments grew heated and the protests sounded. The pity, patience, and the power of uninterrupted love displayed by Jesus in many a troubled scene never ceased to impress.

The colourful, often turbulent, life of Peter serves as a wholesome reminder of the ups and down in our own personal fortunes. We are grateful for the portrait of his warm, rugged personality. Puzzling to himself at times, he wins our admiration as much in his weaker moments as in his show of strength.

We can see at times our own enigmatic selves in the whole gallery of Christians, including the earliest on the list. Not that we can match their bravery and staying power, but we do warm to their companionship and find a touch of kinship when they struggle and falter. The word 'saint' is significantly used in the plural, and only very rarely in the singular, among the early records of scripture and Christian history. The saints were a varied group, but appeared to be reluctant to be isolated. Nor did they bear the title 'saint' as a personal or private honour.

For them sainthood spelt fellowship; saints were

members one of another; good companionship and mutual support, given through love and loyalty, became an important part of their response to God who called them through Christ. They needed each other, just as we need 'human faces' in our joys and sorrows; they serve as signs of God's love and support reflected in all sorts of characters, probable and improbable.

Peter's lost opportunities turned self-confidence into deep and loving trust. He could not find words on the mount of Transfiguration adequate to the occasion, yet he knew it was good to be there. He could not keep awake in Gethsemane, yet that experience never left him. The 'cover up' which drew from him a denial of his Master and one lie after another protesting to his questioner 'I do not know what you are talking about' catches our conscience as well as his. He came through that failure weeping, and repentant. We collapse more often in a crisis, and lose the link with the God who still loves in spite of all. We sense that Peter's training in discipleship was complete when he said to the Master he had let down: 'You know that I love you'. 'You know everything about me'.

Paul

At mid-day, O King, I saw in the way a light from heaven.' In such words the Apostle Paul tells his story. He probably told it many times. It explained everything in his life. The scene on the Damascus road spoke for itself; the incident provided its own argument. An independent, impartial listener, such as King Agrippa, found this spiritual biography strangely moving. As he listened he appeared to be drawn into the issues so convincingly and dramatically described. This story had converting power.

The voice, the light, the pricks of the goad, which jabbed the conscience, all lent atmosphere to the classic description of a catastrophic conversion. The moment was critical; it summed up the past and accounted for the future in the active, afflicted, somewhat tortured life which reached bursting point at noon-day. The conversion of a bully into a champion demonstrated the power released when God encounters an individual and speaks to him in unmistakable accents. He, who had mostly gone his own way 'breathing out threatenings and slaughter' in a programme of persecution, was to find himself strangely committed to serve a community and to die for it, to lose himself in the life of the very Christ he had set out to destroy.

The question, 'Why persecutest thou Me?' brought surrender. He who listened to the voice, saw the light and felt the shame and became a changed person. Struck blind he was made painfully aware in the darkness at noon of his pitiable dependence upon God, the author of life and the giver of light. The blindness which descended upon his eyes, curtained off, as it were, the past, the familiar habits, the traditions and the ambitions of the bad old days. A clear break had been made and the converted one was compelled to start once more at the beginning, obeying elementary instructions, learning from others, through co-operation and patience, what God would call him to do.

He, who was accused of persecuting Jesus when he harried and threatened the friends of Jesus, gave his life forthwith to the Christ whom he was to proclaim in memorable words of mystical devotion, in letters which burned with zeal and passion, in suffering as he interpreted through afflictions and perils the meaning of Christ's crucifixion.

The moment of conversion — in a certain place at a stated time — was not as sudden as it appears at first to be. All that had preceded that noon-tide hour and all that was to follow inspired and explained the work of the finest Christian missionary, the most arresting Christian thinker, and perhaps the most devoted warrior-saint that the Church has ever known.

The sight of Stephen, they say, stirred the vision. The eyes of the spirit perceived the seeds of faith sown by this martyr. The eyes of Saul's head were to be blinded following his threats of slaughter and protests of prejudice. The persecutor was physically humbled and spiritually smitten. Conversion was a growing point. From the turn of the road would follow the maturing of contemplation and the re-thinking of a cultured mind.

There would follow also conflict and pain, struggle and sacrifice. His conversion abruptly begun, continued on many roads and frequent journeyings in the service of the Lord who had made himself fearfully and wonderfully known.

If Saul, now newly-named Paul, found the living God through this experience, he also found himself. Conversion meant a new relationship, a new existence. Nicodemus, who had come to converse with Jesus by night, had also found himself. To be born anew, as indicated by the master, was an existentialist experience. To have a new life involved new commitment and a new relationship with all those near and belonging. A new relationship with God means new relationships all round.

St Paul, in the days before conversion, had found himself through achievements of violence. Like many, he expressed himself fiercely and passionately, with a zeal that turned to jealousy, with a lust for power that shut out from his life the vision of charity and the strength of humility. A new openness was granted to him when his sight returned and the way on was made clear.

The tense moment on the way to Damascus was followed by the prolonged retreat in the deserts of Arabia. Relaxation, contemplation, readjustment and re-orientation brought to the day of conversion a lifetime of renewal.

Martha and Mary

Martha and Mary came from the same home in the village that Jesus visited. Martha, by definition, the mistress and the elder of the two, was the obvious hostess; Mary's welcome was the less obvious. Martha's activism obtrudes; she is distracted with much serving. Out of her large and generous heart, she makes a fuss of her guest, too much fuss, and keeps the house in a flutter. The result is a restlessness, a killing with kindness. Yet there is more to life in the household than doing good; hospitality means more than groaning tables, second helpings and the filling of glasses. There was clearly a clash of personalities revealed in the reaction of the sisters to the arrival of so divine a guest.

Out of the criss-cross of temperaments, Jesus made a memorable point. The domestic scene might well have become a parable, one of those parables, beloved of St Luke, who finds a gospel in the creative tensions of Pharisee and publican, of younger son and elder. Such human scenes remind us that Christianity consists not first and foremost in good works; Christianity is better understood in terms of relationships.

Mary does not appear to have said anything. This did not mean that she was a woman of no importance. On the contrary, as a hostess, she showed her welcome by listening to her guest. At the feet of the acknowledged

Master of truth and life, she sat in the place of understanding. Thus she provided the atmosphere for Jesus to do the work for which he had been sent. This teaching was the most satisfying meat and drink of all. We may puzzle over the exact meaning of the remark, 'One thing is needful; Mary has chosen the good portion'. Some say this meant that one course at the meal was sufficient. Whatever the interpretation, there is no doubt that Mary's way of life is commended as more discerning, more discriminating, as life lived at a deeper level, a life that declares the importance of *being* as well as of *doing*.

We need the blend of the practical and the contemplative. The way of Martha combined with the way of Mary leads us to the vision of God and the true enjoyment of the life he gives us. So we endeavour to fit the season of Lent into one busy programme. Martha did something good; perhaps she overdid it. Mary did something better, but, thanks to Martha, we are able to see beneath the surface to that better thing.

Mary's way helps us to understand 'rest' not as something that takes us away from our work, but encourages us to appreciate that work. Mary's contemplation of the teaching, to which she listened, equipped her to pass on to others the fruits of the contemplation.

The perfect hostess, as she dispenses hospitality, finds joy no less in the receiving than in the giving.

The Friends of Jesus

Y ou are my friends' said Jesus in the famous discourse with his disciples. Friends, he called them significantly, as his destiny and death loomed before them. They were not his slaves. The relationship hung on a voluntary thread.

Slaves generally had little choice of master. Sometimes, however, in the context of compulsion, slaves found a human and friendly response from those set over them. Friends were trusted, with no rules of service to bind them; they could break away from the company of teacher, philosopher and guide.

The friends of Jesus found that they received more than they could ever give. The inspiration, encouragement and initiatives bestowed by the Master astonished them. They had not recognised earlier the possibilities within themselves that he drew from them.

If slaves were the property of their master, they could not call their lives their own. Friendship committed the disciples also with the authority, not of regulations, but of love. There was a perfect freedom to be experienced in the kind of privileged obedience and voluntary service that compelled them to stay in the Master's company.

A delicate situation arose, therefore, for one who was called friend, if with cowardice in his heart he might be tempted not to acknowledge the friendship. An impossible situation it clearly would be for a traitor, who, leaving the beloved community, escaped to a cold lone-liness and the mystery of darkness.

The friendship of Christ was not a one-way movement. Those called into his company soon saw they had something to give in return for the trust placed in them. This relationship with Christ is Christianity. Things done in the name of the Friend and Master surpass the expectation of the doer. His feeble response has strangely effective results. The history of faith is punctuated with the personal triumphs, miraculous achievements and spiritual movements of people who 'built greater than they knew'.

The friends of the Friend have the opportunity of creating a world-wide fellowship. If Christians are friends of Jesus, they are friends of each other. They find they can even love those who are not to their liking. Such friendship is more than human in its expression. These partnerships are threefold in their direction. The God-self-neighbour complex sets the scene for every individual, however eccentric and isolated a personality may be.

Those from the rich mixture of cultures and races in the world of nations have something of their own to show and to be shown in the shadow of Christ's companionship along the way of His truth and life. Could we appreciate the sparkle of the friendship without the laughter of the African Christian? Does not the quietness of the Indian enrich the company and reflect new light from the Master's gifts of friendship? Have we not all something to contribute from the culture in which we are set?

The Ethiopian

The question 'Understandest thou what thou readest?' was put to a traveller on the high road. At some lay-by, as he journeyed south from Jerusalem to his homeland in Ethiopia, a lord of the treasury at the court of his queen, Candace, was found reading from the prophets of Israel about the suffering servant, that somewhat mysterious figure, described as 'a sheep led to the slaughter, like a lamb before her shearers is dumb'.

The Ethiopian grandee is met perchance — some would say providentially — by a simple newly-ordained deacon of the Christian Church, who had been moving through that part of the country with a mission. Philip, one of the specially-selected seven, out to spread the news and influence of his Master, Christ, puts the question to this very important Ethiopian, 'Understandest thou what thou readest?'

It all happened on a journey. The stranger had been to Jerusalem, where was the temple, the scene of the early vision of the prophet Isaiah whose work he was reading. Jerusalem was a capital city, a spiritual centre, where a life of faith was lived and expressed by a covenanted people. The stranger, after his visit, turned south home again; but on the way at the Israel border, in a kind of no-man's land, he reflected and pondered. A question led him to an understanding of an obscure reference from a veiled prophecy. Open-eyed in Gaza, in Philistine country, he came to know Christ for the first time. Travelling a little further along the road, leaving the desert, he found a spring of water in fertile land. He saw that his belief in Christ urged him to belong to Christ. The word of his roadside reading led him to the sacrament of Baptism, into the way of Christ. To understand properly, he must join this life of faith. He must be committed to it, over head and shoulders. There was probably enough water to symbolise the burying of the old way of life for the dusty traveller.

Thus, often do journeys illustrate the marks of the progress, practice and pioneering which characterise the Christian life. The journey to Jerusalem taken by our Lord with his chosen friends was a path of instruction and preparation, and of revelation. As the disciples walked and talked with him, they reached new stages, both geographically and spiritually. The parable of the good Samaritan, also, was the story of a road, told on a road; the road back for the prodigal son was a rake's regress, but a son's progress. The road to Damascus, the pilgrim's path, and the wanderer's way stand for scenes of powerful impacts and spiritual discoveries. Not for nothing was Christianity called the Way. Those who gaze upon the road below, as from a balcony, may think that Christianity has failed; the truth remains that those who have never begun such a journey of commitment, experience and suffering have scarcely discovered the meaning of living by faith.

Patrick

atrick the sinner'. So the national saint describes himself. Yet there is nothing mealy-mouthed about his *Confession*. There is even a modern note of protest in his *Letter* to the soldiers of Coroticus. We are fortunate to have first-hand information about this personality. By reading the two surviving documents, which scholars assert to be authentic and autobiographical, we capture something of the faith and the trials of a dedicated life.

The faith is understood more clearly in our own day when expressed in action. The doctrine of the Incarnation may have a technical, and even a forbidding, sound in the ears of the vigorous young; yet care for the poor, reverence for life, justice for all, regardless of race, colour or creed, are concerns that emerge from a faith that found God in Christ, the Christ who 'though he was rich, became poor, that we through his poverty might be rich'. St Patrick's preaching was patently practical; his love for people pervades his two writings. He moved with a driving force among those who were in need of light and love and life.

This modern ring in his use of the scriptures, and in the personal and immediate application of his faith to everyday life illustrates the lasting nature of a religion that meets human needs whatever the state of civilisation, however great the progress in technical discovery and achievement. When he calls personal ministry 'hunting and fishing', we smile. Such a phrase has in it the realism we are looking for. We smile, we do not deride, for in terms of the wild life, in which he found himself, he searched people out and followed up his approach to them, with a burning desire to banish ignorance and to free them from the fears of superstition. He quotes St Paul's letters with great frequency when he writes his own. The parallel situations made the New Testament teaching about becoming a 'slave of Christ' and 'bringing every thought into captivity to the obedience of Christ' especially vivid in the midst of tyranny and persecution. The fierce times in which he lived served to expound the strength of Christ's pity and the victorious quality of his compassion.

We still need Patrician preaching for our personal spiritual welfare and our common good. The fears within and without, which we all too often feel, can only be overcome by a practising faith that finds God at work through the world, in the very trouble spots and danger zones where the unthinking and unbelieving deem him to be absent. The superstitions of Patrick's day and the knowledge falsely so called were dealt with by a robust humility, with a frank exposure of the saint's own personal problems and obvious shortcomings. If ever there was a living demonstration of the truth in the phrase 'When I am weak, then am I strong', Patrick provided it. His title of 'sinner' in a triumphant life only served to give God the glory.

The saint's personality shines through Patrick's *Confession*. The style and the enthusiasm of this spiritual biography are convincing. Nothing in St Patrick's chequered life is sugared or white-washed. He had close friends and many hundreds of disciples, but he also had enemies and critics. The late Professor Ludwig Bieler's thorough investigation of Ireland's apostle has enabled us to have a vivid portrait of a brave and effective Christian; the example of Patrick's penitence, no less than of his piety, has much to teach us, who find inspiration in remembering him on his day each March, more than fifteen hundred years later.

The *Confession* gives us a glimpse of his spiritual progress. After a troubled start, not without accompanying suffering, he learned about the power of faith in most unlikely surroundings and discouraging conditions. He had not been consistently saintly; far from it. He is honest enough to call himself a sinner. Yet his captivity gave him a vision of spiritual freedom; his readiness to accept the loneliness and misery which slavery involved, produced a new humility. He was not embittered; instead, he found himself maturing under the grim discipline. He was thrown back upon God, and his prayers gained in vitality and love.

He tells of his dreams which soon turned into visions. These revelations of his inner feelings were his own, inimitable experiences. The sinner, who was a saint in the making, is truly human. There is no cardboard character in the story of the *Confession*; Patrick is a flesh-and-blood personality in his struggle for life. He dreamed that he was a stone, fallen from its place on top of the wall, to be stuck in the mud below; only God could lift him out of the mire to freedom and a proper place in life. He saw a ship in his dreams, ready to take him on a journey; later, he heard a voice calling for help, and from such a cry a vision for his whole life and a pressing missionary programme opened up for the dreamer.

We are attracted by the change in him; he relied on God,

rather than on himself. We take comfort from the fear and trembling which he experienced; he drew no one to himself, but as an ambassador for God, with no favourites, he professed the faith. He told his story, with humility and reserve, reluctant to draw gossip on himself, but bold to proclaim what God had done in him and, through him, for the people of the island and far beyond. He did not want to be a bore about himself and his experiences. He only wanted others to learn about the righteousness, as well as the goodness, of God.

Dr Richard Hanson, who made a close study of the Latin language used by Patrick, has published a lively translation of the *Confession* as well as of the saint's surviving *Letter*. From this we become aware that human nature has not changed very much since those days. Personal problems and human relationships were as complex in Patrician times as now; the old solutions of listening, hearing the other side, forgiving, repenting, praying and speaking the truth in public affairs as well as in private communication, still deserve our consideration. We can learn much from Patrick's approach.

A vivid clash of personalities occurs when Patrick, longing to escape from Ireland, where as a teenager he suffered cold and misery, asked the captain of an outward-bound ship for a place on board: 'No way' is the captain's sharp reply, 'No way, you are not to travel with us'. This was a bitter rebuff (Dr Hanson's translation 'No way' for the brusque '*Nequaquam*' dramatises the scene for us superbly).

Soon, however, the captain's tune was to change, when the retreating Patrick, praying the while with silent but determined persistence, rather than resorting to any protest, heard the invitation 'Come back quickly, because these people are calling you. . . . Come on, because we are taking you on trust'.

Such a scene, snatched from the saint's story, shows us that the *Confession* is partly a thanksgiving for a life transformed, and partly a witness to the truth of the gospel. The writer, who had been a slave and quite ignorant of God and his love, was able to talk from the heart about the gifts of freedom and joy in believing which he had received. There is compulsive reading in the writing of this lively saint.

Saint Patrick has been honoured in song, ballad and hymn for centuries. The Book of Armagh, one of the treasured manuscripts in Trinity College Dublin Library, notes the seventeenth of March: the date on which Patrick was translated to the heavenlies. That book, more than eleven hundred years old, also refers to the custom which arose in honour of the national saint, 'always to chant his Gaelic canticle'.

Patrick's *Confession* inspired the later 'Breastplate', a vigorous and triumphant hymn, still sung today. There is much to be learned about the character of a people from the songs they sing of their country and their heritage.

The strong words of the 'Breastplate' express a faith and a courage which we sorely need. To be thankful for Patrick's life and work surely stimulates us to continue in our own time what he nobly attempted and memorably achieved.

He sang 'Christ be with me' and prayed those words also, long before the Breastplate was composed. His *Confession* appears to assure us of this. He thought little of himself and literally lived by faith in the Christ which he came to know in the rough experiences he endured in Ireland.

We rejoice on St Patrick's day, that the saint, who had spent his youth in Ireland as a slave, came back with a spirit of reconciliation and a deep love for the people of this island. A voice called him back; vast numbers were to find new life and a Christian hope through this pilgrim who journeyed among them; this prophet who had a word which triumphed over evil; this personality who was both hated and loved, whose life was marked by both failure and faith, whose attachment to Ireland with 'its whirling winds, and tempests; its glorious sunshine and pale white moonlight', was wholehearted. The beauty and the struggle of life shone through his story of voices and visions, as well as in his dark moments and much else that thwarted him.

Columba

The ninth of June fell on a Sunday in 597 A.D., the year in which Columba died. Every June this remarkable Christian, born at Gartan in Donegal, who has captured the imagination of the nation, is remembered for the sparkle of his personality and the buoyancy of a life packed with incident.

He loved people; he loved animals, too. Many were his good companions in the monastery that bore his name. Full of poetry and vision were his prayers and the psalms he made his own in the island, washed by the waves, where the birds wheeled and a pet crane symbolised his touch with nature and his response to all creatures, great and small.

His Life, written by Adomnán, within one hundred years of Columba's death, is not so much a biography in the formal sense, but rather an appreciation written by a confessed admirer and a kinsman with many delightful human touches which tell us intimately of the man.

In the series of episodes and encounters, the habits and attitudes of the hero are movingly and genuinely reflected. He is given the name 'Columba' or 'dove', writes Adomnán, because of his simplicity and innocence. 'His dove-like disposition offered to the Holy Spirit a dwelling in himself.' His love for God dominates; his longing to share that love with friends and strangers seems to increase, as he wanders about in his pilgrimage for Christ.

He had the gift of keeping in touch with his contemporaries in Ireland, in spite of 'the great spaces of sea and land' which lay between them and him. His constant remembrance of them in his prayers reveals his understanding of their lives and problems.

Often his remarkable anticipation of their needs indicates the depth of his sympathy and his concern for their welfare rather than any specially miraculous foresight. His whole life was radiant with vision; although cut off, in Iona, he sensed what was happening in Durrow, or Derry. If Iona seemed remote and out of this world, Columba made it central through his indomitable faith and the fervour of his vocation to teach, to work and to proclaim the Gospel.

Hospitality was a mark of this love which reached out to others. All sorts among his companions sought him out in the island to which they were drawn in spite of distance and dangers.

Pastorally-minded monastic Ciarán, and academic Comgall, all with their varying interests, reflected the versatility of Columba himself. He had a word for each of them; they called him by a simple, yet perceptive term, 'agreeable'. They declared him to be 'congruous', for they discovered that he fitted in amid their company; his was an empathy that took their problems to his heart.

Concern for others in our day becomes all the more productive, if the spirit of Columba, fuelled by prayer and outgoing love, can stir us to thankful remembrance for the example of such a pioneer. One human failing, in particular, earned his contempt on repeated occasions; he urged his pupils and followers against meanness. This grasping tenaciousness, of which he spoke, was a tight-holding-on to things, regardless of people, a possessiveness and a greed in which there was little love and no caring.

World-wide is not too strong a term for this missionary, who went out from the harbour of his native island, not knowing whither he went. If the journey out from Lough Foyle to Iona's island was a short one, the results of the sailing were far-reaching. 'The dove of the Church' (Colmcille) had a message that travelled over many waters. Those who came and went found the community at Iona a place of prayer, study, and all the resourceful activities associated with a busy community.

The stretch of water that seemed to separate the islands, great and small, off Europe's western coast, proved to be a line of many communications rather than a guarantee of isolation. The words penned in the scriptorium, or writing-room, took wings and spread. The psalter and the gospels, known by heart and pondered daily, when copied diligently in handsome 'island' script, transmitted their message to a distant circumference in the Columban missionary tradition.

The saint wrote until the day of his death with a devotion and a delight in the discipline of his choice.

He turned to his companion, as his strength failed and the quill dropped from his hand, asking that the sentence might be finished and the piece of scripture completed. The last words seemed to serve as a headline for the tradition he founded and would, he prayed, continue. 'They that seek the Lord shall want no manner of thing that is good'.

The saint, who has long left this earth, still inspires. In a very different world, the insights of the community planted in Iona work for peace and mutual understanding in our day.

Columba had successors; outstanding was his humility and his readiness to pass on to others opportunities for progress and even for making history. The great and venerable historian Bede may gloss over Columba's contribution to the story he tells, but he cannot ignore or underestimate the lasting quality of his spiritual leadership and the strength of a tradition which reached out to Northumbria, to many parts of Ireland, and subsequently to the European continent.

This June hero has much to teach us about 'building community and effecting reconciliations', as one of his 20th century admirers, Margaret Cunningham also of County Donegal, never tired of reminding undergraduates, in the university she served.

Ray Davey's vision of a centre of peace-making through prayer and fellowship led to the foundation of the Corrymeela centre at Ballycastle, Co. Antrim, in the 1960s. There were flashes of Columba's inspiration in the development of the community's life during troubled times. The members of this Columban-style fellowship accept the discipline of prayer and work in their life together. They foster harmony among people of varying cultures. They counteract the acids of divisiveness in society with generous love and service.

All Saints

All Saints' Day is a festival of joyful remembrance. All sorts are included in our prayers and reminiscences on this day. The saints with names and places on the regular canonical list have had their days, marked in red, throughout the year. To the select list, we add in heart and mind saints that are known only to a few and those saints that are known as such to God alone. On All Saints' Day, the gap of centuries that appears to divide the classical saints from the present day is bridged; the great day that recalls 'the one communion and fellowship' in the mystical body of Christ our Lord helps to present sanctity as a permanent possibility in the Christian life.

That scene in Rome, when the martyrs of Uganda were honoured, provided a moving example of the fruitfulness of giving formal and official thanks for those who have suffered and died for the faith. In this case, Christians of different traditions and confessions united in honouring the fortitude and triumphant suffering of those who may have worshipped and believed in different ways while they lived, but in the face of death made a similar response to the one God. Death, too often looked upon as a chilly separation, was a powerful unifying force that brought them into a single fellowship. Those who gave thanks for them and continued faithfully to honour their example of living and dying, for decade upon decade, are now able to celebrate together this great act of faith that transcends differences and fosters love among separated brethren.

This martyr story from the end of the last century in Uganda concerns young converts to Christianity in missions, French and English, that were usually rivals in their work. Together, in spite of denominational differences, thirty and more faced the fire to which their chief condemned them. They preferred death to disloyalty to Christ; when they refused to meet the un-Christian demands of their chief, they paid the penalty. All who were present bore witness to the serenity and courage with which they met their death. One visitor standing by the martyr's cross a little way out of Kampala found himself more deeply moved than in any other place on earth. His companion remarked to him there: 'If it came to it, I think the Baganda would be ready to die for Christ to-day; it is living for him that they find difficult'.

All Saints' Day sums up the record of 'the unknown good that rest, in God's still memory folded deep'. All through the year we have had occasion to think of this and that exemplary individual whose name we know, whose deeds are recorded. Some have been favourites for their bravery or their cheerfulness, others for their nationality; most win our affections as much for their human attractions as for their divine enterprises. But on our November feast day, we mention no names, we have no select list. The personalities become merged in the company which moves onward, rank upon rank. There are no historical distinctions, no time-lags; the saints cease to be period pieces; none is old-fashioned nor yet new-fangled. Past, present and future are concentrated here. The timeless poetry of the Sermon on the Mount forms the fitting commentary upon the message of the day. We dwell upon the unspectacular, oddly mild, but deeply influential qualities listed in the Beatitudes. In countless obscure ways the meek, the poor in spirit, the pure in heart, the hungering and the thirsting after righteousness have demonstrated through struggling lives of flesh and blood the blessedness of belonging to the Kingdom of God. The fellowship of 'the bravely dumb that did their deed and scorned to blot it with a name' claims admiration and invites imitation.

We are slow to add names to the lists of saints compiled from long ago. The title 'saint' looks quaint in the pages of modern history. Yet the company and the good fellowship carry their inspiration still. In the roughest situations, the divine pity and the sacrifice of love remain powerful weapons of spiritual warfare. As we praise God 'for all saints' some magnificent contemporaries will surely be in the procession's train, marching beside us. There are modern saints who have broken colour bars, lived victoriously under lock and key, pierced iron curtains, toiled solitarily in this world's spiritual deserts. These unknown warriors have borne witness anonymously and cumulatively to the vitality of the beatitudes of the Lord they have served.

All sorts of saints are remembered at Hallow E'en. This joyful season celebrates life, not death. The birthday of a saint was dated at his or her departure from this life to enter a new and wider life. The joy centred in the fellowship, not in any separation. Lonely people find in All Saints' Day a companionship out of this world.

In the beginning of Christianity every believer was termed a saint. A saint denoted not a type but a real person. All sorts were called to be saints, called to be Christians. All the attractive human qualities would be found in the company: the courageous, the humorous, the intelligent, the trusty and the rest were there. They were not specially known for their mildness or inactivity. There was life in them, and a lively assortment comprised the Church in this or that city, wherever a handful of believers discovered what they had in common and acted as the Spirit moved them. In such company, many found themselves. Beforehand, they had been lost and frustrated. They discovered their identity at the same time as they sensed the urge to share the new life of hope and fulfilment.

The word 'saint' became a technical term in a later age. All Saints' Day has a happy flexibility about its observances. All, whether officially recognised or unofficially belonging, help us to understand the many-coloured qualities of character and the richness of human response to God's love. The saints did not call themselves saints with a capital 'S' as a title; they were aware, all through their lives of love and service, that they were sinners. Constantly they fell short of the glory of God. They assumed new names when they discovered a new way of life; they borrowed names from others who had companied with Jesus and found in the Christian name a symbol of character and reputation. Their identity committed them to a life of belonging, sharing and commitment.

Saints were to be called martyrs; they were witnesses, prepared to suffer death for the truth's sake. As soldiers, they served with a loyalty and courage, militant rather than militaristic. As slaves of a new master, they discovered freedom in a total obedience, voluntarily offered, not tyrannically exacted. If in other days they were called fools for Christ's sake, or God's jugglers, or the Church's underground, such nicknames reflected the nature of a world insensitive to the things of the Spirit. Through protest and eccentricity all sorts of saints, scattered across the centuries, have never ceased to praise God in their lives and by their deaths.

'He was a saintly person, if by saintly we mean possessing the capacity to reassure one about the existence of another world beyond this by simply being what he was'. So wrote a contemporary in a recent biography of a Dubliner. The statement pin-points a feature about sainthood which helps us to appreciate the meaning of All Saints' Day.

There is in a saint's life a unity of purpose which wins popular admiration; there is also in the same life a tension which can readily be understood when we realise that he is a citizen of two worlds.

In our time, the day may mean the celebration of a life offered in a prison yard in Poland in order that another's life should be spared for his family's sake. The day may remind us of the spontaneous generosity of a murdered victim's nearest and dearest, whose thoughts and concerns were given instinctively to another family held in suspense, in the face of a similar tragic bereavement. We shrink from using the word 'sanctity' to indicate the courage and commitment of such unexpected, otherworldly responses. Yet we perceive the touch of the supernatural in these flesh-and-blood scenes of agony and torment. Examples of the goodness which resists vindictiveness, self-pity, and grim bitterness, are produced by more than mere bodily reflexes, active after a sharp shock. Saintliness, however hard to define, is the fruit of faith, and is recognised as a condition of a resilient life, marked by an outstanding capacity for sacrifice. In it are the ever-fresh springs of the Spirit. Saints are not made by accident. Their lives give God the glory.

On All Saints' Day we act supremely as a Church. Our praises and thanksgivings are shared; they span the two worlds to which we belong. 'If anyone believes', writes the Russian Khomiakoff, 'he is in the communion of faith; if he loves, he is in the communion of love; if he prays, he is in the communion of prayer. Therefore, no one can rest his hope on his own prayers and everyone who prays asks the whole Church for intercession'.

A Name for Life

ame this child'. The familiar opening words at a christening set the infant-in-arms at the very centre of the proceedings. The child is the very important person on this occasion; the rest of us are supporters and witnesses of an event which has unseen and unknown consequences.

From the wings, the people present have a faith to share and a hope to express for the future life, now given an identity of a special kind.

We are called by names, not of our own choosing. Some, it is true, reject names selected for them in infancy, and prefer the pet name, or the nickname, or the perfectly reasonable alternative name which has had its own appeal.

Family names give an identity to a child and, furthermore, link him, or her, to a tradition and an inheritance. A sense of life's continuity is felt by those who declare that there has always been a Henry, or a Margaret, or a Dermot, in the family, as each generation passes.

Those who are so-called may, at times, feel inhibited with an obligation, not only to live up to a name, but to live up to and emulate a character, or a personality, not quite one's own. It is difficult, as life proceeds, to separate the name from the nature of the person so labelled. Yet, most find the freedom and independence to claim the name, and to give it a living significance, quite distinct from all the foregoing Henrys and Margarets and Dermots in family folk-lore.

A name, given at a period of history, can date the child; a fashionable name, with a passing popularity, may become a burden, or an embarrassment. Yet we ask what is in a name and find the answer trivial, unless we see beyond the label to the character and influence of the so-called personality.

During their life-time, many have been given names that do, indeed, reveal characteristics. The very ordinary names of James and John were, apparently, exchanged for the powerful collective title 'Boanerges', sons of thunder, for reasons which we may guess. Some names, more seriously, are chosen to indicate vocations and to encourage the following of fine examples of heroism or self-sacrifice. 'A good name', it has been said, 'is rather to be chosen than great riches'. The title of Christ, given to our Lord, indicated a position and royal destiny; the human name Jesus, with its prophetic overtones, pointed to his work and calling of rescuing people and saving them from themselves, their own shortcomings, and all that damaged the life with which they had been entrusted.

In this way, the names of saints have been both fashionable at times, and also inspirational to stimulate growth and progress, and to set a standard for living.

Anonymity is a chill and grey existence; to have no name, and to be unknown may seem desirable for a short time, when publicity blazes and pressures of life and 'other people' overwhelm. Yet, no one is content to be a mere number, a unit in a mighty organisation, or a dropout. Therefore, a name for a child reminds all of us that 'to be' is vastly more significant than 'to have'. Let the name guard the life and give the reputation.